101 God Given KIM*firmations*

Kimberly J. Oliver

Published in Chicago, Illinois by Wealth and Riches Today 1074 West Taylor Street, Suite 335, Chicago, IL 60607.

Wealth and Riches Today is a registered trademark of Wealth and Riches Today, Inc. Chicago, IL 60607. Office: 312.493.4770
Email: lrenee.richardson@wealthandrichestoday.com

Wealth and Riches Today titles may be purchased in bulk for educational, business, fund-raising, or sales promotional use, please email lrenee.richardson@wealthandrichestoday.com.

ISBN: 978-578-67078-2
Library of Congress Cataloging in Publication
Library of Congress Control Number:
Printed in the United States of America

Cover/ Interior Design
Signature Designer: Shirri Buchanan

Signature Photographer: Glen Richardson

2020 First Edition

CHICAGO \\ ATLANTA \\ NEW YORK \\ CAPE TOWN

To

From

Special Note

Foreword

Dr. E. Lorraine Langham

It is not often one comes in contact with someone who, in spite of her circumstances, refuses to let those trials get her down. Meet Kimberly Oliver! Her book, "101 God Given Kimfirmations", is a must-read for all of those desiring a closer walk with Christ, in spite of their trials. I've known Kimberly (I was friends with her mother before she ever married) since her birth. I have watched her grow up in a Christian home and become a woman of faith. She shows us what it really means to live a saved life.

The quotes she gives us in her book: "I may not be high up on your chain, but I'm linked to God" or, "You can't love unconditionally under your conditions" are eye-opening!

"101 God Given Kimfirmations" will not only stimulate you to find God's perfect will in your life, but it will motivate you to say "Yes Lord" to whatever He wants you to do. Like Kimberly, you can become an Evangelist, an entrepreneur, a mentor, an author-- to name a few. Her book, including the testimonies she gives, will help you to be all that God would have you to be.

I highly recommend this book which should be in everyone's library!

Dedications and Thank You

I would like to dedicate "101 God Given KIM*firmations*" to my amazing parents Ruth & Joseph Oliver who are my daily inspiration and the most selfless people I know. I was able to write this book because you loved me in my lane. I love you both with every fiber of my being and enjoy watching the favor of God shine on both of your lives!

"Honour thy father and mother; which is the first commandment with promise;" - Ephesians 6:2

To my late Grandparents – Bishop Percy E. Jordan, Sis. Ella Jordan (maternal), Suff. Bishop Joseph H. Oliver, Sis. Carrie Oliver (paternal) I am grateful and blessed that so many of your qualities, character and legacy live on in me!

To my Godmother Jo-Ann Hite - your years of prayer, godly wisdom and support have guided me on life's journey.

To Tracey Williams my most cherished sister in Christ and anointed confidante who's determination continues to astound me.

To my Aunt Carolyn Mayfield for your kind heart and being one of my biggest cheerleaders in life!

To Nikki McCrary my lifelong childhood best friend since the age of 5 who always has my back

To Pamela Thomas-Henderson whose friendship and spirit of hospitality has been a blessing to my life.

To Etlyn Steele for your continued encouragement and positive outlook in any situation.

To Deborah Silcott my sister-friend who always keeps it real.

To my Goddaughter Mikayla Williams my favorite girl in the world.

To Donald Smith my Big Brother who has been there for me since my childhood years.

To my dearest Aunts, Uncles, Cousins and extended family in the Jordan, Hite & Oliver Families you are loved like you'd never know.

To my late Pastor District Elder Kevin Weeks & The Emmanuel Temple Church Family for my spiritual grounding.

101 God Given KIM*firmations*

I may not be high up on your CHAIN *but I'm* LINKED *to God.*

You can't love
UNCONDITIONALLY
under your own
CONDITIONS

Life KICKED *you to the* CURB *but* God *said you will* WALK *the* STREETS *of gold.*

Don't trust someone's "I told you so" *over what* "God told you so!"

Holiness is not a LOOK

it's a LIFE.

People can only star in your show if you allow them onto your set.

You can't RAIN *on my parade I'm already* SHOWERED *with blessings.*

I'm open for Kingdom Business.

I can't afford to be on your SCHEDULE *and miss my* APPOINTMENT *with* DESTINY.

Don't settle for a

TITLE *that makes*

you compromise

your POSITION.

Don't worry about who wrote you off as long your name is written in the Lamb's book of life.

You can't pull the WOOL *over my eyes because I'm following the Good* SHEPHERD.

Don't dive into your FEARS.

Take a LEAP *of Faith.*

The SUN *rises because the*

SON *rose!*

No one can steal your THUNDER *if you don't share your* FORECAST.

You don't have to throw me any BONES. *I'm too busy feasting off the* CRUMBS *from the master's table.*

If you put all of your EGGS *in one basket you* SCRAMBLE *your options.*

Let people see the GOD *in you not the* GOSSIP *in you.*

Don't PARK on Acts 2:38 unless your life is DRIVEN in Jesus Name.

If you're on the HIGHWAY *to Heaven you'll stand the test when the rubber meets the road.*

Putting your TWO CENTS *in will never* ADD *up to the favor of God.*

The big fish in a little POND *mentality will get you* SWALLOWED *up when the enemy comes in like a* FLOOD.

When your hands are TIED,
LOOSE *your*
Holy Ghost!

Jesus endured OPPOSITION *to change our sin sick* CONDITION *not for pulpit* RECOGNITION.

It's not enough just be
SPIRITUAL *if you're not*
SPIRIT FILLED.

You can't OUTSHINE me
I'm abiding under the
SHADOW of the Almighty.

You don't have to SIT *in sin.*
Stand UP *for Christ.*

Stop playing the NUMBERS
and COUNT *your blessings.*

I'm not BRAINWASHED

I'm BLOODWASHED.

Don't RULE *with an iron fist then* BREAK *the golden rule.*

Make the MOST *out of your journey and the* LEAST *of your current situation.*

You'll feel much better if you take the chip off of your SHOULDER *and let it roll off your* BACK.

Make it a point not to ROLL *with people who won't* ROLL *up their sleeves and help you.*

People might be INSENSITIVE *to your circumstance but you serve a God who can make* SENSE *of your circumstance.*

You don't need an extreme MAKEOVER *you just need an encounter with the* MAKER.

Make sure you're barking up the right TREE *your blessing could be in the* BUSH.

Never trust a PALM *reading over the* HANDS *of God.*

Take Jesus out of your POCKET *and serve Him in the* OPEN.

You don't have to RUB *shoulders just* BOW *to the King of Kings.*

Stop SPINNING *your* WHEELS *and turn to God.*

You dropped me like a hot POTATO *but God picked me up and turned me into golden* FRIES.

When you stay under someone's thumb you allow them to crush your spirit.

God gives us a FRESH *word*

don't give Him a

STALE *praise.*

When you have God the BEST *is with you at your* WORST.

Eat your humble PIE *on earth*

if you want a SLICE *of*

Heaven.

Stop sugar coating the word of God. The Bible doesn't need any frosting.

You can't give it your ALL *until your* ALL *is on the Altar.*

Once you fully SURRENDER *you won't have to live your life as a* PRETENDER.

From PATIENCE *to* PERFECTION *in Him.*

Let God FILL *your*

EMPTY *promises.*

My season isn't coming.
It's already here.

God will take you from being STRESSED *out to being* BLESSED *out of your mind.*

Love is not a STATUS *it's a* STATE *of mind.*

Cupid's AIM *is off; God's love is your best* SHOT.

I'm going on FAITH *not* FACT.

Yokes are broken when the talent show ends and the anointing kicks in.

Stop trying to SOLVE *your problems and let God* ABSOLVE *them.*

When folks turn their BACKS *on you,* FACE *Jesus.*

Occupying a pew doesn't guarantee that you will occupy Heaven.

Love never STOPS. *It* STARTS *with God.*

Don't let someone else's
NIGHTMARE *frighten the*
DREAM *out of you.*

A CRISIS *calls for Christ!*

Stop doing YOU *and do God!*

You don't CATCH *the Holy Ghost you* RECEIVE *it.*

Some people LOVE *to* HATE *and* HATE *to* LOVE. *Let's* LOVE *the* HATE *out of them.*

Keep LIVING *for God*
because He DIED *for you.*

You'll never be FREE *living independent of God.*

The Holy Ghost is our license
to operate in
Jesus Name.

God STEPS *in when people*

WALK *out.*

You can't BOTTLE *up your praise and expect God to* POUR *out His blessings.*

When you LINE *up with your assignment from God He will set the record* STRAIGHT.

You're not 2nd *choice*
because God chose you 1st.

You are not your STATUS.
You RANK *in the Kingdom of God.*

It's not WHO *you know it's*

WHOSE *you are.*

Don't let anyone make you FEEL *like who they think you are.* BE *what God said you are.*

It's not who's watching me...it's who's watching OVER *me.*

Don't trade you

HALLELUJAH *for a* HUSTLE.

Your PRAISE *outweighs your*

PAY.

Your OBEDIENCE *unto God yields much more than a big* AUDIENCE.

Why are you trying to CONJURE *up what God told you to* STIR *up?*

You are not STUCK *you are* ROOTED.

I didn't FALL *off the radar.*
I soared above it.

God's love is RIGHT *even if someone* LEFT.

God's not PUNISHING *you*
He's POLISHING *you.*

Sometimes you don't realize how close you are to your farthest dream.

People will drop the BALL *but God will put a* BOUNCE *in your spirit.*

Don't settle for sloppy seconds when God gave you first dibs.

You won't spend an ETERNITY *in Heaven treating God like a Time-Share on earth.*

Don't BEG *God.*

OBEY *God.*

Never expect people who aren't up FRONT *with you to have your* BACK.

Feelings are driven by EMOTION. *Relationships are driven by* DEVOTION.

Live RIGHT *so you can*

LEAVE *right.*

An UNFORGIVEABLE *act is*

no excuse for an

UNLOVEABLE *response.*

Praise is not a PHASE *you go through. Praise is what takes you* THROUGH!

Life GOES *on but love* LIVES

on.

I may not be in the LOOP
but I'm on the STRAIGHT
AND NARROW.

There's nothing SANE *about* SIN.

The power of God will make you STAY *when you want to* RUN.

Even when you don't FEEL *like it.* BE *like it.*

Make sure you don't just feel GOOD. *Make sure you feel* GOD.

AUTHOR CONTACT

KJOLIVER30@AOL.COM

Printed in Great Britain
by Amazon